From Jack & Margaret Brown
to Jim & Rosemary Crawley 1975.

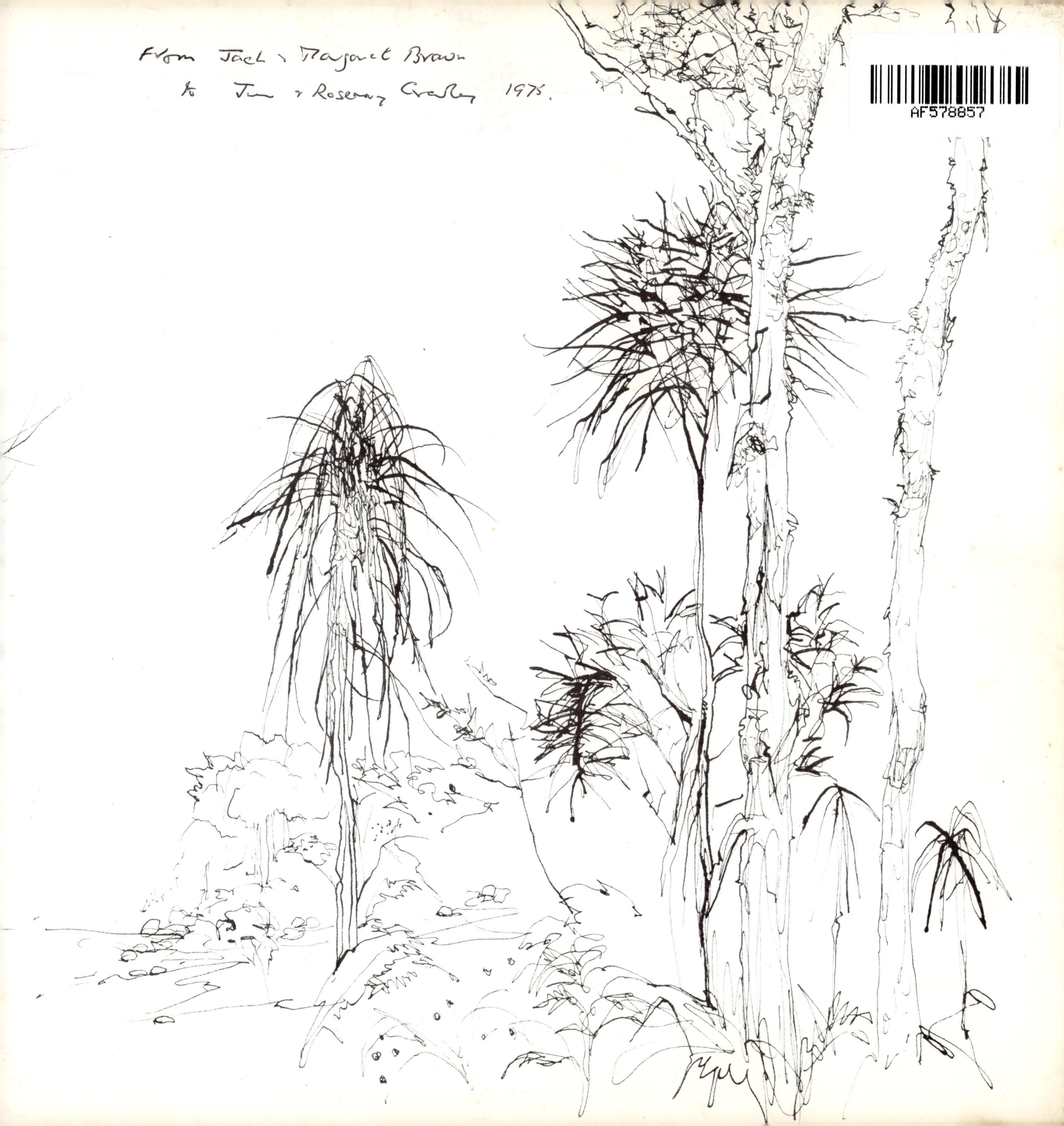

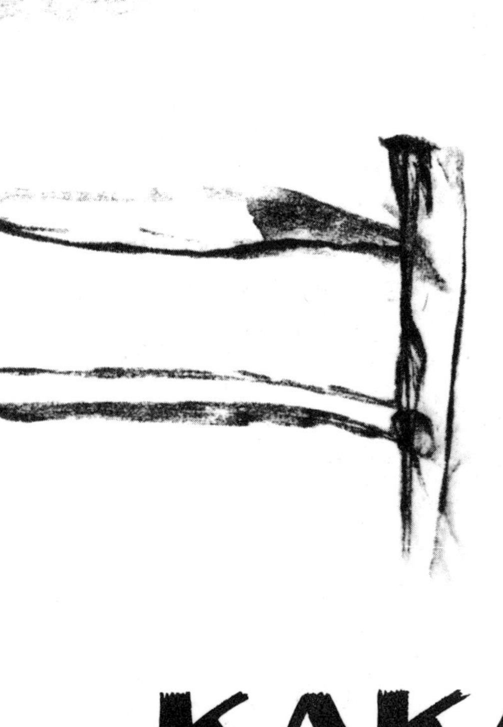

KAKAHI
NEW ZEALAND

Looking towards Kakahi from above the Wanganui River. My cottage is on the edge of the bush in the mid-distance.

KAKAHI NEW ZEALAND

PETER McINTYRE

A. H.& A. W. REED
Wellington . Sydney . London

First published 1972

A. H. & A. W. REED LTD

182 Wakefield Street, Wellington
51 Whiting Street, Artarmon, Sydney
111 Southampton Row, London WC1
also
29 Dacre Street, Auckland
165 Cashel Street, Christchurch

ISBN 0 589 00742 4

Set in 14/16 Plantin by Consolidated Press Holdings Ltd., Wellington.
Printed and bound by Kyodo Printing Company Ltd. Tokyo.

To Sara and Simon

Cattle being driven across the Whakapapa River.

FOREWORD

YEARS AGO, my old friend Ted Webber (*You Should Have Been Here On Thursday*) asked me and my family to come fishing at a place called Kakahi in the King Country. I had never heard of it.

That was nearly thirteen years ago and today Kakahi is a part of my existence, woven into the fabric of my family life, and I have Ted and Kathy Webber to thank for it.

I know every pool on its miles of river, every track in the surrounding bush. It has been my escape and my hideout from an ever more strident and ugly world, my refuge from the inane persecution of the telephone. It has restored my faith in this world as a place to live in and has brought to me, like heaped-up riches, the beauty of the bush and rivers of my country, New Zealand, for Kakahi *is* New Zealand.

This book is the story and the picture of Kakahi, the village, the river and the people.

PETER MCINTYRE.

ACKNOWLEDGMENT

I am extremely grateful to the editors of the *Kakahi School Jubilee Magazine*, from which I obtained so much of the information about the history of Kakahi, and would like to convey to them my sincere thanks.

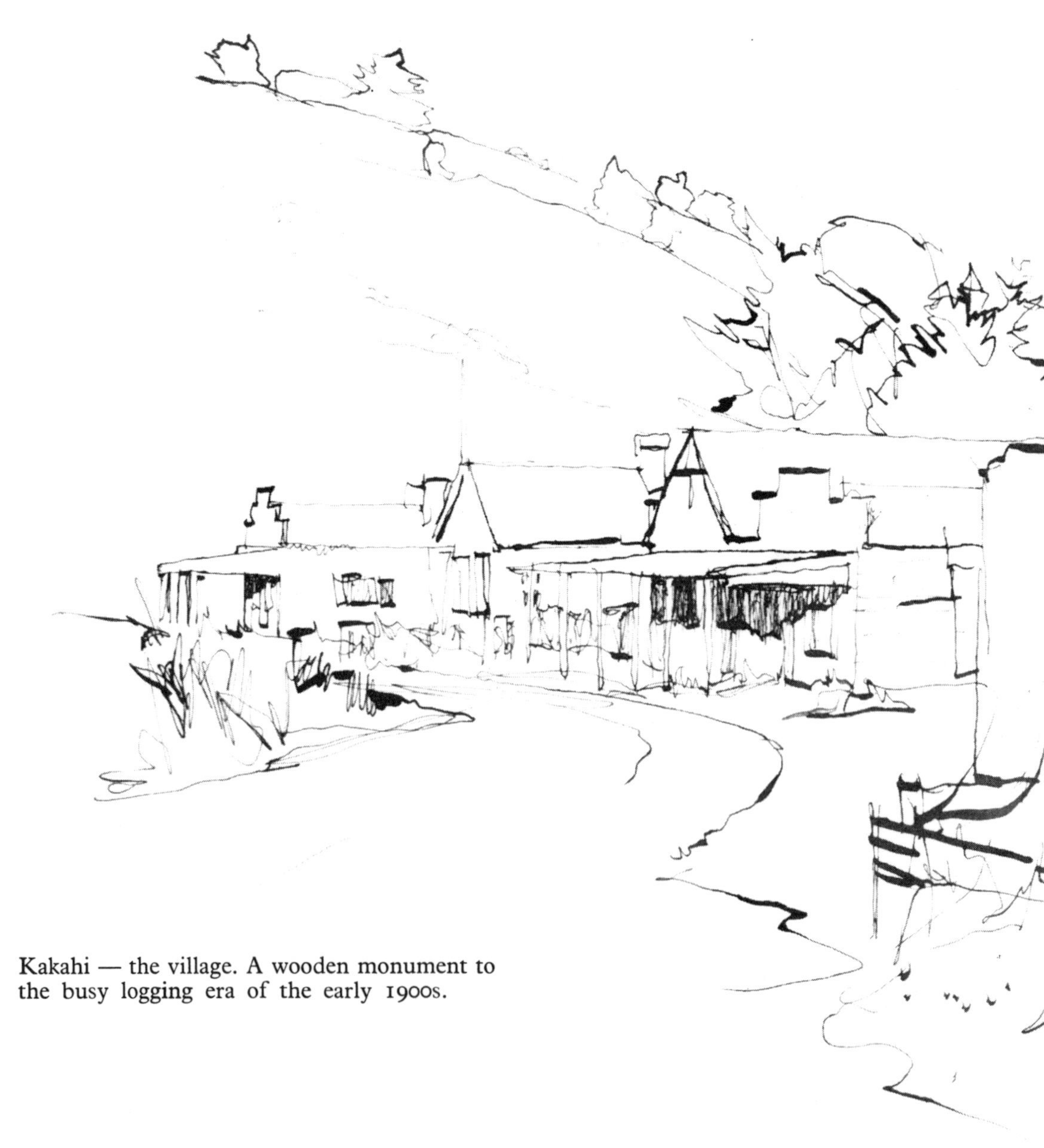

Kakahi — the village. A wooden monument to the busy logging era of the early 1900s.

Maori girls. Behind their shyness lies a Polynesian beauty very similar to that of the Tahitians.

THE COLOUR PLATES

Late afternoon from the verandah of the Hurley cottage on the edge of the village.

PLATE I: Looking toward the bush and the mountains from the edge of the village, a scene that evokes the quiet peace of the King Country.

Old hitching post. The horses are mostly gone now and there's no need to hitch a Land Rover, but how much more pleasing the horses must have looked.

KAKAHI

THE NAME KAKAHI DERIVES FROM THE FRESH-water mussels found by the early Maoris, in the stream that flows through the village. Kakahi meaning, simply, mussels.

Kakahi is a King Country village. It isn't much of a village really; a few old false-fronted shops, an abandoned post office and a horse-hitching rail no longer used.

The false-fronted shops have the look of a Western movie set, as so many seedy little towns in New Zealand do. Maori boys riding bareback on shaggy horses sometimes add a touch of colour.

There's a Maori pa over on the outskirts; except for the church the pa is built in the old, classic concept of the earliest pas, with its meeting house and houses around a marae.

Not much happens there now, but when they built the meeting house in 1913 tribal representatives came from all over New Zealand for the great hui that opened it. It was called Wharepuni Taumaihiorangi, after the house of Toroirangi, a tribal ancestor.

Much of the life of the pa has faded now as the young men leave to go off with the shearing gangs or to drive a bulldozer over at Taupo.

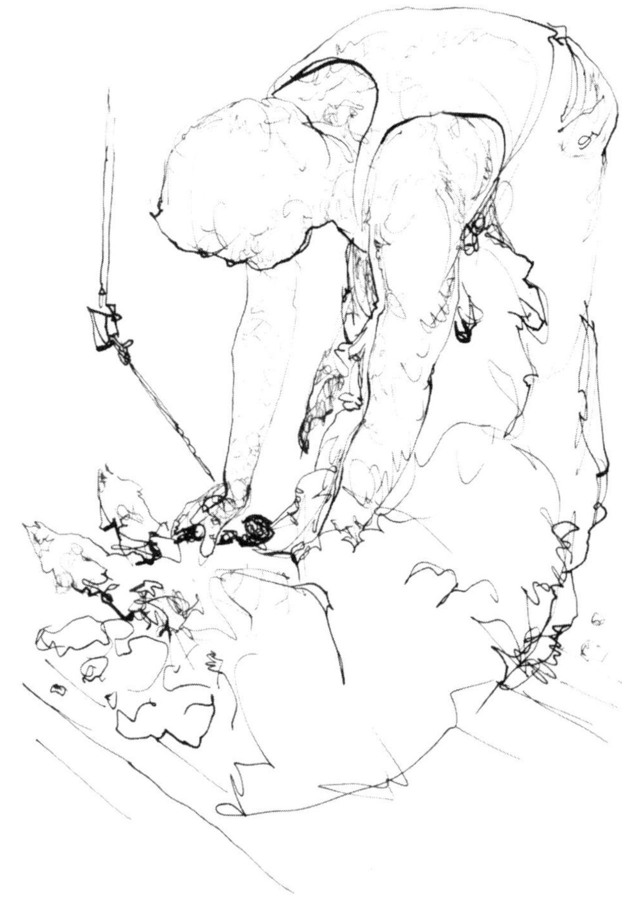

From up on the hillside above the river, Ngauruhoe sends up a plume of smoke on the evening air.

PLATE 2: The church and a glimpse of the marae seen from behind the meetinghouse. This meetinghouse was opened in 1913 with a great hui, and tribal representatives came from all over New Zealand. It was called Taumaihiorango, after a tribal ancestor.

A Maori son of Kakahi.

But Kakahi has something not often found in New Zealand places—it has a sense of history that makes more than just a village and a pa. It has a personality all its own, distinct but indefinable, as of a person who has seen much of life. For the story of Kakahi goes right back to the fifteenth century.

There is a small stream where you come into the village whose Maori name is the key to the history of Kakahi, as it goes directly back to the great Battle of the Five Forts that was fought here between the Whanganui Maoris and the local Ngati-Hotu tribe somewhere around the year 1450.

After the battle, the victorious Whanganui Maoris hung the legs of the Ngati-Hotu dead on poles in the forks of the trees—the final insult to an enemy who broke and ran. The name of the stream is Whataraparapa — "the hanging (of the legs) in a line".

The Maoris, having no written language, handed down their family and tribal history from father to son, generation after generation, in the same way as was done in Hawaii and in Tahiti. This custom continued until European-style education and the written word put an end to it. Unfortunately, little of the old

tribal history was recorded, but luckily we do have the story of Kakahi.

The Takiwa family, still living in Kakahi, is directly descended from Turangi-Toa-Tahi, one of the three chiefs who fought in the Battle of the Five Forts on the Whanganui Maori side. Some years ago, Takiwa Tauarua told me the story of the battle, a story handed down to him through fifteen generations.

Takiwa Tauarua spoke no English, but his story was translated by his son Hohepa Takiwa.

The original people living at Kakahi were the Ngati-Hoti, a tribe of the Tangata Whenua who had been discovered by the Arawas living around Taupo and Roto-Aira. They had been defeated at the Battle of Puke-Ka-Kiore Mountain and killed or scattered.

Apparently some of the remnants had gathered near what is now Kakahi and, safe from outside attack for some time, had increased in numbers. It has been claimed that the Ngati-Hotu were a prehistoric or pre-Maori people. Maori tradition says that they were fair-skinned with reddish golden hair. In describing them the great Maori chief Te Heu Heu Tukino used

Every boy seems to ride some shaggy nag. Wild horses used to be plentiful in the area.

Our cottage on the hilltop
above the Whakapapa river.

the words kiriwhero, meaning reddish skin, and Urukehu, meaning reddish-golden hair.

It does seem faintly possible that these people were the remnants of some migration that took place before recorded Pacific history, even before the time of Kupe.

After the battle the few remnants fled into the Patea country and vanished from history.

Takiwa Tauarua's story of the battle tells how the Whanganui Maoris, exploring up the river, found these people living where the Whakapapa and the Wanganui River join; a place I see downstream from the lawn of my cottage.

The Ngati-Hotu were in such numbers that the two chiefs with the exploring party, Te-Ka-Pe-Iti and Turanga-Toa-Tahi, sent a messenger back for reinforcements. Eventually a third chief, Te Hoata, arrived with a war party.

The Ngati-Hotu had set up a ring of five forts around Kakahi and until only a few years ago there were traces of the earthworks where the fort called Takapuna stood on a steep hill above Mr Gray's farm near the village.

Sometimes when fishing a pool of the Whakapapa in the

Kingfisher

evening, I look up at the hill where Takapuna stood, and somehow the fifteenth century doesn't seem so far away in time.

One fort, called Otu-Taarua, was on the clifftop behind the church at the pa, some 200 feet above where the river flowed until the floods changed its course, while another called Ariki-Pakewa was directly across the river.

An elderly Maori once pointed out a burial mound to me across the river.

"The chiefs are packed in there like sardines," he said.

On the classic divide-and-destroy principle, the forts were attacked and taken one by one. Te Hoatu took Kakahi fort, where Ryan's slaughteryards were located in recent years.

Re-Ka-Pe-Iti and Turanga-Toa-Tahi took Otu-Taarua, attacking across the land where the pa now stands, and finally Ariki-Pakewa was taken.

The final bloody phase of the battle was fought out on the flats between Kakahi and the river.

PLATE 3: Ngauruhoe sends up its plume of smoke on the winter morning air heralding, according to Kakahi tradition, fine weather. In 1926 and again in 1956 the mountain in violent eruption was an awesome sight from the village.

It was than that the limbs were hung on poles set in the forks of the trees and the stream was named Whataraparapa, a name that has survived in Kakahi for over 500 years.

On a hill near the village there is a great heap of stones. Some local Maoris believe them to be the remains of the hangi where some of the Ngati-Hotu were cooked and eaten.

Until the Main Trunk railway line came through, the King Country was forbidden territory to the white man, its name coming from the fact that it was reserved for the Maoris under their Maori King. To them it was known as the Rohe Potae.

With the coming of the construction gangs, however, a calico tent town sprang up where the Whakapapa Road now runs above the river from Owhango to Kakahi. This tent town with its attendant merchants and hangers-on grew until it had several pub-shanties and a gambling den that was notorious but so well guarded that it was never raided. This town became known as The Holy City and survived until 1905, when it was destroyed in a great bush fire, the residents saving themselves by fleeing into the railway cuttings.

Until a few years ago, a heap of bricks, the remains of the baker's oven, lay by the roadside, the last reminder of The Holy City.

The weathered face of the old Kakahi smithy.

For years after the railway came, the King Country roads were dustbowls in summer and mudholes in winter.

Sir Carl Smith of Dunedin, who was once a schoolteacher in the King Country, told me that on one occasion when he was bringing his wife back from hospital with a new baby son the buggy wheel sank so deep in the mud that mother and child were thrown out.

On another occasion, his wife got out to help push the buggy and lost her shoes in the mud — she never did find them again.

For many years the King Country was legally "dry", although it is said that in most places the church was about the only building in which you could not buy liquor.

It is significant that the King Country became "dry" at the request of the Maori chiefs — not from the white man's concern for the Maori.

In 1884 the Taumarunui chief, Haki-Aha-Tawhiao, petitioned Parliament that intoxicating liquor be excluded from the area. A proclamation was issued forbidding the sale of intoxicating liquor and by 1908 the King Country Licensing Act was passed.

When the King Country finally went "wet" the nearest pub to Kakahi was at Owhango. It was a very small place, but on opening night they had six policemen on duty outside.

King Country evening on the river.

PLATE 4: The village at dawn. The first rays of the morning sun light the facade of old shops. With its haunting sense of time past it sits with a seedy charm like a Western movie set awaiting the actors.

Ray Bennett with his horse and dog.

THE MOUNTAINS

FROM KAKAHI on a fine day the three mountains — Tongariro, Ngauruhoe and Ruapehu — loom up over the bush-covered ridges across the southern horizon, often spectacular in a covering of winter snow. It becomes a habit to look for the plume of smoke from Ngauruhoe — somehow it seems to set the mood of the day since the mountains, although distant, exert a dominating presence over the whole area. It is easy to understand that to the Maori the mountains have the significance of an ancestor — you feel their presence almost as that of a living person.

In 1886 there was great fear among the Maoris that the mountains might be cut up and sold piece by piece to one person or another thus destroying their *tapu*. As the great Maori chief Te Heu Heu Tukino said, "Tongariro is my ancestor, my *tupuna*; it is my head; my *mana* centres around Tongariro. My fathers bones lie there today."

Thus, in 1887 Te Heu Heu Tukino and all the other chiefs of the Ngati Tuwharetoa presented the mountains to the nation for all time.

Ngauruhoe erupting, seen over the ridges from the village. The mountain, dominating the southern horizon, is regarded as an ancestor by the Maoris.

Sometimes from Kakahi we have seen Ngauruhoe perform in spectacular fashion, sending up great mushrooms of smoke like the explosion of an atom bomb. At others, Ruapehu has erupted disastrously, filling the Whakapapa River with grey mud and ash, so loaded with toxic poisons that thousands of trout have been killed. After the eruption of several years ago, dead trout littered the riverbank for sixteen miles above and below Kakahi.

The bush that was the glory of the King Country.

PLATE 5: Local farmer Ray Bennett bringing a mob of sheep down a bush track.

KAKAHI TOWN HALL
Gaytime
De RESZKE

Old loggers' bridge over the Whakapapa.

THE LOGGING ERA

WITH THE RAILWAY came the sawmills and the great logging era of the King Country. It was also the end of some of the most magnificent and beautiful forest in the whole world. Great totara and rimu were felled in thousands and teams of draught horses dragged the logs across the river to the mills. The old smithy where the horses were shod still stands in Kakahi and I have painted it for this book.

On Whakapapa Island, between the two rivers below my cottage at Kakahi, there remains one stand of the original bush, all the rest being second growth, risen in the forty to fifty years since the bush was logged.

To walk in that stand of the old bush is to walk in a cathedral where the sunlight cuts in shafts through the green half-light as though from high Gothic windows. As evening comes and the light dims, the bellbirds and tuis' sound their notes from tree to tree until the whole glade echoes a fabulous evensong.

When, some fifty years ago, the Wilson family of Wanganui built a summer cottage here on the Whakapapa, Mrs Wilson asked the loggers to leave that one glade of trees as a sample of the original bush, and so it stands today.

At that time there was such a vast acreage of bush that few people gave a thought to its destruction. Today, with the area of remaining bush ever dwindling, the destruction still goes on, with the bulldozers leaving great scars of clay across the hill-faces.

At the height of the logging period, Kakahi had a population of over 600 people. There were two boarding houses, a billiard saloon and a picture theatre — the local pianist playing the accompaniment to silent films twice a week. Rudolph Valentino had come to Kakahi.

Every Friday night there was a dance in the Town Hall and once a year a great social event, the bachelors' Ball. The "Merry Five" orchestra of five local residents — three violins, piano and drums — was kept very busy with the round of social events. Horses stood tethered at the hitching rail and every evening groups of men stood gossiping outside the billiard saloon.

Music was taught by Mrs Humphries and Mr Linthorne.

There were a number of performers who helped make the

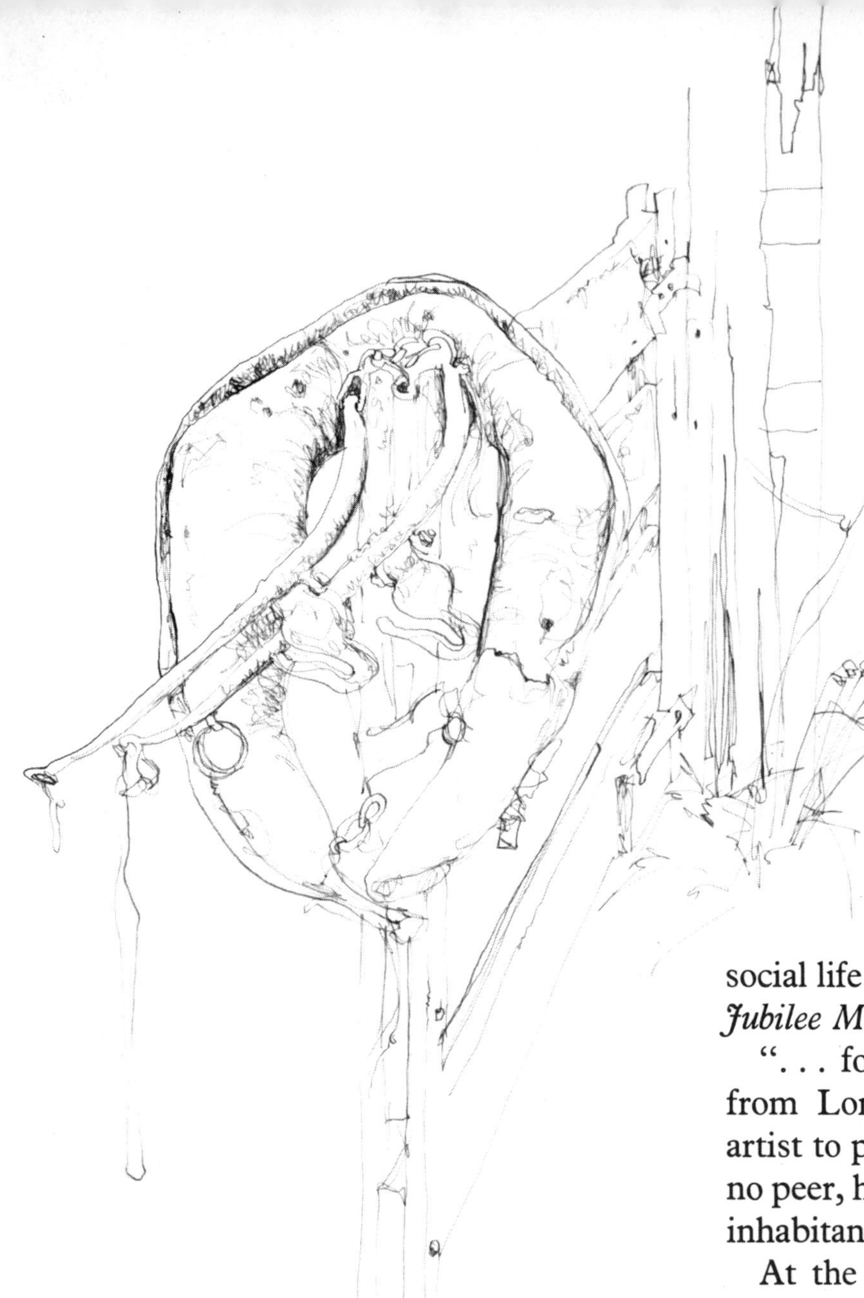

Old harness that still hangs in what was the blacksmith's shop.

social life of the village and here I quote from the *Kakahi School Jubilee Magazine:*

"... for instance — Miss Sarah Moreby then not far away from London's greatest concert hall and probably the finest artist to perform in Kakahi. Mrs Arthur Mudford, another with no peer, her golden voice thrilling hundreds of those first-decade inhabitants of Kakahi."

At the dance, apparently, a Mrs Greenstreet of ample proportions was frequently asked to dance by a tiny man "noted for his obsession for dancing with ladies of Mrs Greenstreet's stature".

On one occasion when the little man booked her for a dance, Mrs Greenstreet arranged for the pianist to play a particularly long waltz, seized the little man and held him at arms' length for the duration with his feet a foot or so off the ground.

Another performer was Mr Goldfinch, who recited his own poems and had toured with the New Zealand Nigger Minstrel Troupe (*sic*).

His poems included *Up in an Aeroplane Lads!*, *The Bushman*, and *The Navy*. His song and act '*Black Billy's Dream*' was

PLATE 6: Old smithy. This was the blacksmith's shop back in the days when the logs were dragged across the river by teams of Clydesdale horses. Oldtimers remember Mr Le Prou, the blacksmith, and horses called Baldy, Monte, Duke and Nugget.

The bush. Fortunately some native bush was kept as a reserve on the edge of the village adding much to the charm of Kakahi.

“applauded in New Zealand, Australia and England”.

Today if you pass through Kakahi any time after dusk you will not see a soul. The cinema is gone, the Town Hall is closed, and under the street lamps only the many prowling cats are visible: the human beings are hidden away in their houses watching *Coronation Street*.

All over the world, as in Kakahi this decline in village social life is taking place, a sort of cutting-off of social contact. Except for odd momentary meetings in the store, there is no longer any common meeting place, no conversation, no exchange of thought, no building of friendships, nor the stimulating drama of hatreds.

Yet, comes a summer day and the village nestles in a peacefulness the agonised outside world has lost.

The old smithy where Mr Le Prou shod the Clydesdale horses still stands but with the silent weathered look of old age, and mosses grow on old wooden rails.

Out beyond the village, old concrete foundations and a vast heap of sawdust are all that is left to mark the sawmilling days. The sawdust is said to be forever burning inside, and sometimes when the wind blows it bursts into flames.

Maori boy. Happy with all the carefree ways of his race: but he'll probably be gone to the city before he's twenty.

PLATE 7: Maori children at the pa. Few children in the world have such carefree happiness and shy charm. Often they are quite beautiful, but sadly most of them drift away to the towns in their late teens. The ties and the disciplines of the old tribal life are gone without replacement.

"The cutting." Dug in the early 1920s for a railway that never made it. It was to have connected Kakahi with Taupo.

THE CUTTING

PAST THE CHURCH a dusty pumice road leads out across the flat where the last phase of the ancient battle was fought and down through the railway cutting to the river. The cutting is a reminder of a futile attempt to build a railway from Kakahi to Taupo for the timber trade back in the early 1920s. For years, heaps of rails and sleepers lay beside the river, but that is as far as the railway ever came.

The cutting is deep with vertical pumice banks lined with ferns, making an eerie half-light inside, even on the brightest days. At night myriads of glow-worms make the walls look like a city seen from a plane at night. It is one of the star after-dinner entertainments for our English and American visitors.

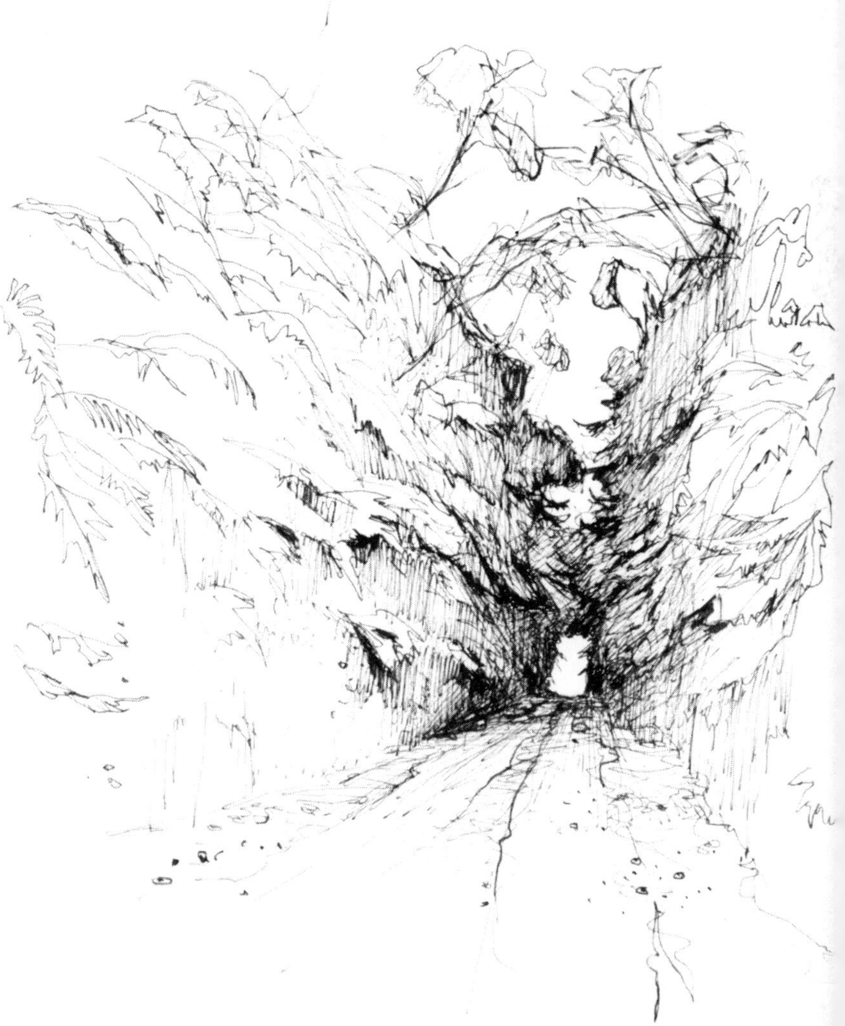

At night the cutting twinkles with a myriad glow-worms.

My neighbour, farmer Mr Ham, in his fields.

PLATE 8: From the lawn of my cottage the early morning mists roll and tumble across the river.

A Kakahi summer day with Patti, Simon and our dog Curry off across the bridge to Whakapapa Island.

THE BRIDGE

MY COTTAGE is on an obscure dirt track off this road and sometimes visitors miss the turn-off. They go down through the cutting, which is awesome enough, and come to the log bridge which, as they think they have to cross it, literally scares hell out of them. As one of them was heard to say: "My God, look! There are *wheel* marks on to it!"

Built by the loggers, the bridge consists of four huge logs placed with one end on the bank and the other tethered by cables to a sort of rock island in mid-river. The idea is that the floods that sweep with ever increasing force as more bush is cleared will go not only under but over it. When the loggers ceased to use it, the bridge became more and more decrepit. The logs sank in places and reared up in others until the angles of the decking became ever more hazardous. The floods swept away pieces of decking and these were replaced with bits and pieces until the whole affair took on a crazy Heath-Robinson look.

It was one of our more sadistic sports with guests, especially from abroad, to drive them through the cutting and nonchalantly proceed to drive across the bridge. Usually they made a last-minute jump for it. Some wouldn't even walk across, and one woman stood on the bank and covered her eyes while I

Maori children.

Old abandoned barn. All around Kakahi one finds these old places, so quiet that they seem haunted as no doubt they are.

bumped across, but I should mention that a tall fragile English girl sat calmly beside me as we lurched and bumped above the swirling river, telling me about her pet parrot.

Ed Landells, an American friend of mine, when asked if he'd rather walk said, "Hell no. If I'm gonna go, I'm gonna go." To heaven, I think he meant.

My daughter says she saw a Maori woman, a friend of ours, crossing the bridge in a pick-up with her eleven children all over it, even up on the roof of the cab. Halfway over, she reached up and banged her hand on the cab roof. "Hey, you kids, you better hang on," she said, as a sort of afterthought.

Yet once when a small child fell off the bridge into the deep water where it swirls in a whirlpool underneath, the same woman, Polly, jumped in and came up with the child. Polly can't swim. A sheepdog that fell into the same pool swirled around until it drowned.

Sadly, only a short time ago the floods came and one morning half the bridge was gone and with it our access to all the lovely places on Whakapapa Island, to the swimming holes and the upper reaches of the Wanganui River.

PLATE 9: As dusk falls ever the King Country, dead stumps rear tortured limbs in protest against the evening sky. Below, where a branch of the Whakapapa makes a first meeting with the Wanganui, the shadows enfold an old favourite swimming pool, and in nostalgia I can almost hear the voices of so many summer days.

Old swing bridge over the Wanganui. A few years ago it was still in use and used to set up such a bouncing that it almost threw you in the river if you tried to walk across too fast.

THE RIVER

TO ME, living in a country of fast-disappearing wilderness, and seeing lovely old favourite places turned into something like a Glasgow public park, Kakahi was at last a place where we could explore and wander, where the beauty and charm were provided by Nature, not Nature organised by man.

Across Whakapapa Island we found a great long pool with a sandy beach sheltered by bush on one side and with high papa cliffs on the other. At its head the river cascaded in to give swimmers a ride down to the long calm stretch. No speedboats were needed to pull them, and above all there were no speedboats to turn the summer day into a roaring horror.

There we could grill a trout on the bank for lunch, loll and swim the day away in a setting of dreamlike beauty.

There seems no end to the moods and joys of the river from the early morning when the river fog eddies and lifts, making islands of treetops and suspending ridges in the sky, to the heat of the day when the bush on the faces is azure blue in the heat haze. I have seen the river mist at night with the moonlight coming through it to create a vast and awesome stage setting of gently moving gauze curtains.

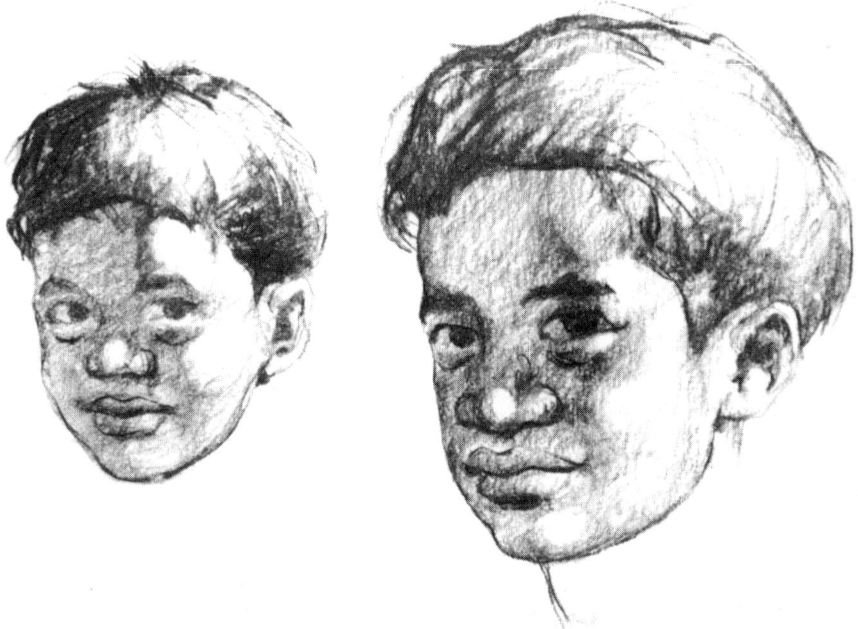

This summer from my lawn I watched some Maori children floating down the river on old inner tubes, on a log, and in one case on an old copper hot-water cylinder. They were like a gaggle of geese, but shouting and laughing, hurtling down rapids apparently without fear right down into the big rapids of the Wanganui.

I said to my wife that I wished I could do that.

"Why don't you try?" she said, looking at me sideways and leaving me with a suspicion colder than the water.

Exploring up the river we found bush tracks that led up into the headwaters of the Wanganui, into bush so wild, so tall and awesome, that in there one seems to be a tiny Gulliver on a planet of giants.

Sometimes I've heard deer just ahead of me in the bush. As long as they don't see you they seem to take you for some other animal and do little more than snort and move nervously, but at the merest glimpse through the trees they are off like a flash of light.

Each pool on the river has its character. The long stretch at Macdonald's, for instance, is a pool to be fished when just in a fishing mood, without any great ambition to catch anything.

It flows smoothly and quietly; it is easy to fish, and it has the

Maori boys of the village.

Pukeko.

interest of its birds, from pukekos to paradise ducks. The paradise set up home among the boulders there and keep up a great racket of distraction when a fisherman comes casting his way down the river.

This pool, like so many others, has its lie; an exact spot where the fish seem to be in wait for food, for a caddis nymph or a moth of some sort. Everyone in the family knows that as you fish down this pool you are most likely to get a strike exactly below a certain tree. It sends a tingling through the scalp when you have worked down the pool until the fly is coming round at just that spot.

Turner's, as another pool on the Whakapapa is called, is a difficult pool, to be fished when one is in a mood to cast expertly and calmly. Here the fish rise far over under the opposite bank so that a long, long cast with a dry fly is necessary, across the current at that, but when on the rare occasion that everything goes right and the fish visibly takes the fly to set your reel screaming, then that is the most rewarding moment of all.

PLATE 10: The Whakapapa River emerges from the gorge below Owhango. On the right the main trunk railway cuts around the hillside. This picture was painted from near the site of the Holy City, as the notorious tent town that came with the railway-building gangs was called. In the early bushfires, people sheltered in the railway cuttings above the gorge.

Like most males I tend to fish the tried and true places, but my wife Pattie adopts the feminine approach and fishes the most unlikely places on the whole river. She catches more fish than anyone else. It makes me feel that we males might do better at many things if we forgot occasionally about our much prized logic and let our instincts have a go. Women's Lib can have that one, for what it's worth.

Trout, of course, are gloriously unpredictable, which gives them a certain affinity to women and possibly explains my wife's success. Comes the evening when conditions are perfect. You rush to the river quivering in anticipation and that is the very evening when not one fish will rise, when your fly goes over and over a pool with not a touch and it seems that all the fish must be dead; but comes an evening when the river is dirty from rain and the wind is howling upstream — that's when the big one hits your fly, when you're so unprepared that you're left with nothing but a broken cast and a bitter soul.

At the age of five my son Simon began to learn to cast a fly. At eight he caught his first fish — it was probably the unluckiest trout in the Whakapapa and very small indeed, but he caught it and all that day his face was one large grin .

Recently I watched him, seventeen by now, play a magnificent fish that ran his line out to the backing over and again before he landed it. I have also seen him learn to be philosophical about fish that he's lost at that heartbreaking moment of landing after a long, long struggle.

One of our dachshunds, even, got interested in fishing. He would stand on the bank watching the water intently and bark at the rising fish, giving direction by pointing his nose — a sort of fish-pointer. My wife has caught fish by casting in the direction he pointed.

Pools on the river began to be given names for sheer family convenience of identification in conversation, so we have the Junction, the Scree, Macdonald's, Cooper's and the Big Hole, dotted over some ten miles or so of river.

It makes a wonderful end to a summer day when we all come in from fishing various parts of the river, each with his or her tale and nobody exactly listening to the other.

It is extraordinary how differently one thinks when on the river. Thoughts seem to come with a clarity that is impossible in a house or on a street with their television sets, telephones, radios, cars and, worst of all, people.

I would have been as sceptical as any about Victorian moralising on the enobling and purifying thoughts induced by Nature;

but it cannot be denied that, by the calm of a lonely pool, surrounded by the green of giant trees, thoughts rise above the trivia of dislikes and irritations, of petty worries. I suspect that my only worthwhile self-appraisals have been made there on the river in the loneliness of evening.

An artist's life is generally a happy and rewarding one, but in the later years that I have reached, one tends to think more of what one *might* have achieved than of the more-or-less doubtful successes of the past. All my working life each picture was going to be the one that would at last achieve something, yet inevitably it fell short of it and in the end a sense of frustration hovers like a cloud. Yet here on the river I tend to think that life has been good, that even for me there is still much to be done. Above all, the years here with my wife and children have been the best fulfilment of all.

I have been intrigued to note how the ways of fishing tend to follow the temperament of the fisherman. Manu, who runs the store and does everything with a quiet restraint, fishes with short casts, never trying to get great distance, never attempting too much, but he moves across the river boulders like a mountain

PLATE 11: A pool on the Wanganui, the scene for my family and their cousins of so many summer days.

PETER McINTYRE

goat, covering every eddy, dropping a fly behind every stone.

Simon, with his youthful ambition, casts so far that most of the time he's fishing the other side of the river.

Mr Christianson, who lives in the village, fishes without moving much but goes on long after dark with great patience.

Mr Inglis fishes the same pool night after night.

Pattie, on the other hand, picks a side stream that looks as though no self-respecting trout would live in it, casts under willows among snags and comes home with a couple of beauties and an air of one who is nobly saving a lazy family from starvation.

Ted Webber, who writes very funny fishing books such as *You Should Have Been Here On Thursday*, fishes with a sort of bulldog determination and a conviction that the trout are "having him on", which is probably true. He also refuses to acknowledge the fact that the boulders are very slippery and frequently falls in. Once, when crossing the river ahead of him I looked round and saw nothing but the top of his hat. He surfaced with the water cascading off him all round so that he looked exactly like a garden fountain.

"You should have been here on Thursday," I said.

The wild goats are another feature of the riverside and the bush. All sizes and colours, they come down to the river to drink and then toward evening they can be seen grazing their way up through the clearings. A year or so ago, a small herd became established on the wrong side of the river, that is, on our side, and caused havoc among Pattie's precious plants.

They were led by a massive great billy with a long beard and a fine spread of horns. Simon went after them, but the old billy showed a cunning unusual in a goat and always led his herd into the bush at the gallop along obscure paths. He seemed to sense approach before he could possibly have seen the hunter.

It developed into a sort of vendetta, a game of wits. Once Simon got a shot at the big one and knocked him clean off his feet, but he was up and off in a second.

Finally in near darkness one evening he came out into the clear without his usual sense of danger and that was his end.

His horns measured twenty-eight inches across, but for all the damage he had done we all felt a strange sense of loss.

My daughter, Sara, for all her femininity, went off into the bush on her own and accounted for another of the herd, and since then the garden has not been invaded.

Head of a billygoat. He brought his herd into our garden and caused havoc, so my son Simon swore to shoot him. The old goat was so cunning that it took months, but finally Simon got a shot at him and this is the trophy. Span of horns: 28 inches.

Customers at the Kakahi store.

PLATE 12: Maori girls. Shy, and aloof, and full of what dreams. Getting to know these children is a little like getting a bird to feed from your hand.

The store. Here you can buy anything from a rifle to a raisin. Manu and Kamu have retained the old style casual, personal touch that died elsewhere with the advent of the supermarket.

On the steps of the store a typical group waits as usual for nothing in particular. Kakahi is one of the few places left where you can settle down to doing absolutely nothing with pleasure.

THE STORE

WITH THE CINEMA GONE, the billiard saloon gone, the Town Hall closed, the bakery closed and the sawmills gone, almost the entire social life of Kakahi centres around the store. And now that the post office has been incorporated — in a small back room — the store has become the only live nerve centre in the village.

In its way it is a sort of Aladdin's Cave, festooned with the minor treasures of modern life — pitchforks and paperbacks, shirts and spades, newspapers, magazines, fruit and fishing flies. Its literature ranges from *The Guns of Navarone* to the *Kama Sutra*. In winter there is an old potbellied stove to warm your knees. In America you would see an exact replica of the whole scene in a Norman Rockwell painting.

The mail arrives mid-morning: the Auckland paper may arrive or it may not, in fact in holiday time the odds against its arrival increase to the point where no Kakahi man would take a bet. The outside world doesn't matter very much here, anyway.

The real news is right here, brought to the store and dis-

Kamu

tributed by word of mouth and then by party-line telephone. By the way, I have heard of some Maori families holding a religious service complete with singing on the party-line.

The news that matters is who shot a deer this morning, that someone blocked Jimmy Spier's gate and he couldn't get his hay away; that David Johnston is getting married.

The store and the post office are run by my friends Manu Lala and his beautiful wife Kamu, with tact, patience, politeness and a quiet sense of humour — traits not nearly as plentiful as the goods in most of the bigger stores in more "civilised" places.

We have been saddened by the long illness of Manu's father, Dahya, who used to run the store. We miss his quiet dignity and his pleasantness.

There is something of a cosmopolitan touch to Kakahi with its European, Maori and Indian mixture.

Manu once managed to get my son Simon on to the local cricket team for a game, as eleventh man. At the time I think he was aged eleven. I was intrigued to see Simon going off in Manu's car — Manu immaculate in white flannels, Simon extremely scruffy in his holiday clothes and Manu's mother, who speaks no English, beside them in her long sari.

When I asked Simon what team they had played, he said it was "Her Majesty's Prison" and that they were nice men who had bowled him "softies" as he was so much younger than the rest of the team.

It is in the store that one meets the personalities and the characters of the village. There is Rosie and her husband Mac, the hardest-working farmer I know, for ever bringing another field into production out of a wilderness of scrub and blackberries. There is Mrs Long, the retired postmistress, who makes jam and marmalade she doesn't want, for the sheer joy of making it. She presents many jars of it to my wife, together with jars of pickled onions. There is Mr Ham, my farmer neighbour with his kindly ways and beautiful Maori voice. There is my old friend Dick Barnett. Although sorely crippled I have seen him putting in fencing posts and moving from one post-hole to the next on his hands. His is the most outstanding example of sheer courage that I know. There is Jimmy Spiers, a Scot who has lived all over the world, speaks Russian and German and

Manu

Old potbellied stove in the store.

prefers the quiet of Kakahi to any place on earth. There are the Allen twins, as alike as two peas, and their wives who are sisters. There are Bennetts from across the river, Dempseys and Johnstons who farm on the outskirts of the village, our good friends Polly Te Ahuru and her husband, and a swarm of Maori children, Te Ahurus, Mahus, Hamipos, Hams and Takiwas, whose ancestors were here long before the white man discovered New Zealand, to say nothing of Kakahi.

I find it difficult to understand why so little is acknowledged of the great history and background of the Maori people. Here are people whose ancestry can be traced directly back for five hundred years and more in New Zealand's history, yet it seems to be scarcely noticed while Christchurch, for instance, makes so much of its First Four Ships.

At school I learned much about Abel Tasman and Captain Cook but practically nothing about the arrival of the great Maori canoes whose occupants must have been among the greatest sailors and navigators of all time.

Surely a greater consciousness of their own great heritage would give that much needed sense of status to these same shy children of Kakahi.

Sonny Te Ahuru, a Maori friend of mine, member of a fine wellknown local family.

The cottage seen from across the Wanganui River. The Wilson cottage is to the right in the trees.

PLATE 13: The Whakapapa at dusk. In the twilight the river catches the last light from the evening sky as it winds to join the Wanganui. The hill in the left mid-distance was the site of Takapuna, one of the five forts that fell in the battle against the Wanganui Maoris back about 1450.

Looking towards the headwaters of the Wanganui River from my lawn. Taupo is beyond the horizon.

The Walford house from the river. It was originally the home of Greg Kelly, who writes about this very pool in his book *The Flies in my Hat*.

THE COTTAGE

WHILE OUR CHILDREN were still of pre-school age, we had gone to Taupo for holidays, always leaving before the influx of the school holidays. But at last we were caught in the ratrace, perched perilously on the edge of the gin circuit. We began to feel that we might as well try to holiday in a suburb.

Salvation came when my old friend Ted Webber with whom I'd been in North Africa and Italy asked us over to Kakahi, a place I had never heard of. With a final round of gins we packed and left Taupo. We never went back.

The road from Tokaanu over to Taumaranui passes through some very beautiful bush with a unique view across at Ngauruhoe and Ruapehu, and I began to shake off the depression of Taupo. From the highest point of the road I looked out across the country ahead, mile after mile of ranges receding into blue distance, and my first view of the King Country.

I think I was sold on it from that moment. Here was the sense of freedom that comes with distance. This was the last part of New Zealand to be "civilised" by the white man and somehow it seems to have retained something of that spirit of wilderness.

The old Wilson cottage with the owl on the gatepost. Carved many years ago by Mr Wilson, its presence on the gatepost denotes family in residence.

PLATE: 14 Dipping. The Johnston farm lies on the outskirts of the village and here David Johnston and a neighbour work a long hot day putting the sheep through the trough.

Here is a place where the bush seems to grow taller, more lush and green than anywhere else; where the foliage makes a green twilight beneath even on the brightest day. This also was the fortress of the notorious Hauhau whose great wooden crosses could be found deep in the bush until only a few years ago.

I found the Webbers in the old Wilson cottage, a place set in tall trees above the Whakapapa River. It was late afternoon and the cliffs above the junction of the Whakapapa and the Wanganui were lit in a blaze of afternoon sun. Wild goats were feeding on the grassy slopes; the tuis were sounding their notes in the bush and the sighing sound of the river seemed to fill the summer air.

When the Wilson family first built their holiday cottage and came for holidays here, it took them eight hours by train and horse and cart from Wanganui. They tell me that in those days when the train stopped at National Park, all the passengers got off to throw stones at the rabbits. There were so many you just couldn't miss.

In those days there were salmon in the river, and Larry Wilson told me of seeing a fish in the river so large that at first he presumed it was a log until it began to move upstream. On another occasion he was watching a duck with its young on a

pool when suddenly a great snout came up and a duckling disappeared in a swirl.

The water must have been too warm in summer and after a year or two the salmon disappeared, but for some years once in a while someone would report hooking a trout so large that it was probably a stray salmon returned from the sea.

For some years the trout fishing was very good all along the Wanganui above Taumaranui, and in the Whakapapa Gorge near Ruapehu fish up to twenty pounds were taken. But the disastrous eruptions of Ruapehu with their poisonous mud and ash have killed so many fish and destroyed the caddis fly and other feed. In fact, in the year after the 1945 eruption exactly one fish was taken from the Whakapapa.

This year (1972) the headwaters of the Whakapapa will be diverted to the Tongariro Hydro Scheme and what could have been one of the world's best fly-fishing rivers will probably be ruined. New Zealand is not yet aware of the value of its rivers, of its wonderful heritage; they are still the stamping ground of the philistine.

Incidentally, three of the best-known trout flies in New Zealand — the Twilight Beauty, the Kakahi Queen and the Pessie —

were designed at Kakahi by the then local postmaster, Mr Basil Humphrey.

This information came from Greg Kelly whose books, *Gun in the Case, Gun in the Hills* and *Flies in My Hat* are so well known. Greg discovered Kakahi many years ago and built his house above the river. It was he who first brought Ted Webber fishing here, so indirectly I owe my happy years at Kakahi to Greg as well as to Ted.

After two summers in the Wilson cottage I knew that after all my wanderings around the world I had found the place I wanted. I bought a piece of land and with my neighbour, John Walford, as carpenter and myself as builder's labourer, we built a cottage, a sort of A-house with one leg lifted.

Inside I based it on an old London studio with a musician's gallery for the children to sleep in and a big deep verandah where we practically live in the hot King Country summer. From my lawn I see nothing but bush and river for miles — not a red roof in sight.

I built a studio in the garden and from its window I look across to a long pool in the river under the bush where the eddies

PLATE 15: The Anglican church, and beyond it the old smithy in the brooding twilight. It is a place of peace, unconcerned with time.

Twelve years ago, the deer would cross the river beside us as we fished. Today they are few, killed off by the meathunters for export. True, they damage the bush, yet nobody seems to worry about the opposums that destroy so much more.

catch the sun and sparkle like moving crystals. Sometimes the sparkle comes from a rising trout.

From just before dawn the birdsong begins, for in that still moment just before the first light becomes apparent, the tuis in the bush below begin with a single bell-like note. By day, fantails flutter all around and this year two bellbirds raised a family in a nest in a kanuka on the edge of the lawn, while later two pheasants hatched chicks in the barley field at the back of the cottage.

Kakahi, and particularly the country around it with its river, makes a perfect miniature New Zealand; a sort of preservation of so much that was best in this country, a reminder of a New Zealand that is rapidly disappearing.

Since we came to Kakahi, my work has taken me all around the Pacific; through more than 20,000 miles of the American West; to Canada and Alaska. I have enjoyed all the luxuries and pleasures the wealth of America can give, yet through it all I have longed to be back at Kakahi.

I am one of those fortunate fishermen whose wife also fishes and so we have had endless pleasant evenings together on the river.

Deer shooting expedition from Kakahi.

We have had those happiest of all years here — the ones when the children are with us through the holidays — the idyllic days of exploring the river, of picnics by the swimming holes, of fishing and shooting over miles of river and bush. This is what Kakahi has given me, something that is uniquely New Zealand, that could not be bought or equalled anywhere else in the world.

The world today is rapidly becoming an impossible place to live in, a jangling chamber of horrors in which man is like a cornered animal beset by every form of nerve-shattering torture ranging from ceaseless noise to pollution, bashings and incomprehensible income-tax forms.

Already cities such as New York have become uninhabitable except for those who cannot escape, and the blight is rapidly spreading. Man worshipped Progress but slowly he is realising that it is a false god, not only the cause of his troubles but likely to hasten him to ultimate disaster and self-destruction. Pollution alone has become a monster problem and a mortal danger to the continuation of human life.

In this situation New Zealand has become one of the last havens of refuge, and the whole tortured world is turning an

envious eye on us. Everywhere I go in America people who a few years ago wouldn't have known where New Zealand is, tell me how much they want to come here. Many want to retire here.

Yet in New Zealand we still have the old "progress" mentality. We still have local bodies that will find any excuse to chop down a tree, to bulldoze native bush.

"You can't have trees, there's drains everywhere," as the mayor of one of our cities said.

We have a Government that uses a "do it first; ask the public after it's too late" method to push through schemes that will ruin some of the world's most beautiful places and New Zealand's greatest assets for the sake of a bit more hydro power.

Thus we seem determined to turn a country whose one real distinction is its unique beauty and grandeur into a commonplace dreary little imitation of countries already ruined by the disasters of progress.

PLATE 16: Old abandoned houses like this are almost a symbol of the King Country, gazing with the sightless stare of empty windows to hills rising above the winter morning mists. In this one an ancient long black dress with white lace collar and cuffs still hangs in a dusty cupboard.

My studio looks down on this scene on the Whakapapa.

Places such as Kakahi may seem to be going backwards, even to be dying, but in a civilisation faced with disaster this may well be what will ultimately save them. At least in Kakahi much of what makes life worth living has been preserved; its countryside has retained some of the beauty that made New Zealand unique.

I trust that this book will record something of the New Zealand I have known and loved and that for my daughter and my son it will be for all their lives a reminder of many happy days at Kakahi.